When Bruised Reeds Break

a book on restoration

Returning a life to the destiny God intended

Danny Steyne

Forewords by Jack Taylor & Randy Clark

Published by MOWBooks

mow

"...another book about what Jesus did..."
John 21:25

When Bruised Reeds Break
Copyright ©2005 by Danny Steyne

Scripture references are taken from the Holy Bible, New International Version Copyright © 1973, 1978, 1984 International Bible Society, Colorado Springs, Colorado

Published by:

MOWBooks
P.O. Box 212204
Columbia SC 29221-2204
www.MountainOfWorship.com
worship@MountainOfWorship.com
803-665-8990

MOWBooks is a ministry of Mountain Of Worship, a South Carolina non-profit organization dedicated to perpetuate the event of sustained, perpetual lifestyle worship of Jesus that releases a heavenly demonstration that causes the lost to bow their knee and the found to adore the One they live for ... until every knee bows ... until every tongue tells ... both the lost and the found ... in heaven and in hell ... that JESUS is Lord!

ISBN 1-59196-992-1

Printed in the United States of America
For Worldwide Distribution

Dedication

She walked into my life at the time of greatest pain. I was resigned to loneliness, I was resigned to brokenness... but God had something so much better for me... He planned for restoration and I fell in love with His restoration plan... Karen. You were the first glimpse of restoration for my life, you have walked me through so much personal restoration, and helped me to see the God who loves to restore. What He has done in us is nothing short of miraculous Grace... you are my best friend, my confidant, my beloved, my bride and the love of my life... I am so thankful for you. This book is dedicated to you because you demonstrate to me daily that God loves to restore... and you are the evidence of that!

He does not crush the
weak, Or quench the
smallest hope; He will
end all conflict with his
final victory, And his
name shall be the hope
Of all the world."

(Matthew 12:20-21)

Acknowledgments

I would like to extend a special thanks to all those who helped me through the process of this book. Some of you are a part of this story; others remain a hope that I carry in my heart that you will experience His restoration and power. All of you have helped immensely. Thanks especially to Mark & Nicole Odom... my friends who understand the value and grace of restoration. Thanks. Thanks also to my parents, Phil & Jeanne Steyne who carried me through many of those dark nights when it seemed as if all abandoned me. Thanks to the many pastors and leaders who encouraged me to write this volume. Thanks also to those at Mountain Of Worship who helped with all the editorial and art comments. Thanks especially to my brother Paul, who asked me the hardest questions.

ఠ‍ుౖ

Endorsements

The first time I set eyes on Danny Steyne he was sitting at a table in his church in North Carolina, and was deep in prayer with a colleague. From that first day, I have had the greatest respect for Danny and for his ministry of worship. In this book, Danny takes the calculated risk of being transparent and brutally honest. He exposes the fact that there is a lack of the spiritual among us who are able to restore the fallen and the hurting, but that there is a plethora of Job's comforters who cloud the counsel of God with words without knowledge! This book will help us understand that the evidence of our spirituality is not in our ability to judge and condemn, but in our ability and willingness to restore.

Jack McKee
New Life Ministries
Northern Ireland

Danny is one of the most real people I have ever known. He is caught in the destiny of restoration of individuals in a church world that is in a season of major reformation. In the crucible of pain, brokenness and real forgiveness transforms the pain into real love, Resentment of the pain and those who have been used to inflict it produces bitterness and a life void of love. This book presses us toward the process of reformation from religious ways into the pure holy love of the Father. Danny's no nonsense straight forward way of presenting the truth and real life experience will touch the broken and take them toward restoration and it will touch and challenge leaders toward reformation of church into the manifest loving presence of God.

Ron McGatlin
Coordinator OpenHeaven.com IRN CRC
Mt. Airy, North Carolina

Danny Steyne is the real deal. He has been knocked down, but never knocked out. From the trials of life, he has emerged as a great warrior for the Lord—a testimony of God's mighty grace. Because Danny has endured the fires of adversity and brokenness, he now offers you pure gold, the riches of God's kingdom.

Jim Buchan
Crosslink Ministries
Charlotte, North Carolina

I've known Danny Steyne for a long time and have always appreciated his calling and giftings. To say this book is timely is a gross understatement. The church's past and present is riddled with the broken hearts and lives of many of its once great leaders. I trust that Danny's experience and message will be a wake-up call for our generation to mobilize and become a healing and restoring community. This book is invaluable for all who have been bruised or will minister to bruised reeds."

Gary Oates
Dallas, GA
Author, *Open My Eyes, Lord*

Danny Steyne has gone through many crushings and pressings, and has come through the crucible of life with the compassion and authority to be able comfort others with the comfort God has given to him. His story will bring you to a new understanding of the love and grace of Jesus Christ through life's trials, and bring to you renewed hope.

Joni Ames
ACTS Ministries
Charlotte, North Carolina

Danny has dealt with one of the Church's problems, that "we (the church) shoot our wounded." His statement, "The Church has simply wanted converts that make no mistakes....and walk through life 'clean'" cut my heart to the quick. He deals with the reality that we share the good news of restoration with the lost and broken, but extend little grace to believers who do not measure up to our expectations.

Thanks Danny for sharing your story, your pain, and your journey to restoration of your destiny. I believe this book will enlighten many to our false expectations of "perfect believers" and lead them to extend grace to those in the body of Christ who need it most, those broken reeds.

I have found Danny to be a grace giver and encourager, in his brokenness, he experienced the Father's restoration, and now he is a vessel of that power to restore.

Ron Fearneyhough
Pastor, Gracewood UMC
Augusta, Georgia

This book "When Bruised Reed's break" written by my friend Danny Steyne reveals the deepest failing today in the church. The lack of understanding of how to restore and bless those who have been wounded and broken is one of the most painful experiences I have had to learn. Often the church receives and extends love conditionally. I am grateful that there is hope in the Lord Jesus Christ for all who have failed, been broken or poured out whether through sin, self inflicted suffering or moral failure. He will restore the broken hearted unconditionally and that is the truth.

Danny shares how to be Spirit led in restoring those who have failed and have suffered much pain. For the church to be Kingdom minded and effective in restoration this truth needs to be learned and the scars received from the experience need to be revealed to a dying generation of people who have lost their way to restoration because of religion and rejection.

Ron Campbell
Sound the Trumpet Ministries
Grapevine, Texas

Our cities, our nations and our churches need men like Danny Steyne who tell the hard experiential journey into and out of discouragement, brokenness, and rejection. Men who live because they dared believe they could again be used and impact the destinies of others. Danny Steyne and those like him see the Samson's of today and know they have one great miracle of God left in them. Danny sees the Peter's of tomorrow and knows that despite the ultimate sin of denying the Christ there is a kingdom being established through them. Danny speaks to the David's who despite moral failure, depression and discouragement are used to birth a Song of Songs and a book of wisdom for the ages. Danny knows his subject well. He has walked it out. He calls us to the promises of greatness we all carry despite our failures. The grace that is ours, the hope for tomorrow, the reality of One who is always, always faithful, always loving and the ultimate lover of our soul.

David Van Cronkhite
Blood 'N Fire
Atlanta, Georgia

This book will reach deep into your spirit and soul. As you travel through life with Danny, you will laugh and cry, to only find joy in the process of forgiveness. Once you begin, you will not be able to put this book down. If you have been bruised and broken, this is an excellent book to read. It is health for your soul.

Phil Dowdy
Senior Pastor, New Life Family Center
Elizabeth City, North Carolina

Danny Steyne knows, perhaps more than most of us, the pain of trials. To his credit he didn't become bitter, but has retained a peace and joy that comes through an intimate walk with God. He has something of importance to say to each of us as we face rejection and judgment by those that we loved. Danny came out victorious and lights up the path for others who walk the same road. This book shares a depth of understanding in dealing with trials that lead to total dependence on God. It will bless and strengthen the lives of all who read it.

Glenn Anderson
Pastor At Large, Forest Drive Church
Columbia, South Carolina

ॐ

Contents

൭൦

FOREWORD

BY RANDY CLARK

Danny Steyne's book, "When Bruised Reeds Break,"
is the best book for expressing the heart of God for
broken people I have ever read. It is a moving story
through which we learn about the weakness of the
Church in knowing how to restore those who have
experienced the breakdown of the family, and
those who have fallen in general.

I was moved to tears as I read Danny's story, and was very impressed that one who had been so wounded by the Church could reflect such maturity and compassion for the Church. I was reminded of my favorite college professor who asked me the question when I was about 20, "Randy, do you love the Church of Jesus Christ enough to serve her when she hurts you?" I said, "Yes!" Within two years I would be tested.

I too personally understand the need for the Church to improve in how it cares for its wounded. I applaud Danny for his courage, honesty, and love for the Church and those who belong to it who are bruised reeds. May his book teach us how to better reflect the heart of our Savior who did not break the bruised reed or put out a smoldering wick. Danny has written an excellent book. I highly recommend this book to every pastor, elder, deacon, and anyone else wondering about the heart of God and the issues pertaining to restoration.

Randy Clark
Global Awakening Ministries
International Conference Speaker, Author
Brazil, 2004

ഇഇ

FOREWORD

BY JACK TAYLOR

Thank you for giving me the privilege of an early reading "When Bruised Reeds Break." I write many endorsements, prefaces, and introductions and I do not recall many books to which I refer as a "must-read." But yours is one I would include in this short list of "must reads"!

I generally browse a book, pick up the drift, and

central message, and respond to that. This procedure was impossible with your book. I found a shallow and casual reading impossible. I knew something of your story and never failed to pray when I read references to it (sometimes with weeping). I have suffered from recent stunning and crushing losses but they seem to pale before what you have experienced. How God must love you and what He must have planned for you.

Your mixture of personal sharing of feelings with relevant Scripture references is very appropriate and helpful to so many of us.

It is a story that, when read, touches all of us at some point of need, pain or fear. This is a story about loss and betrayal covered by grace and forgiveness. The goal is easily detected in the early part of the book: the restoring of lives to one another and to God as well as the restoring of joy amid darkness and uncertainty. It is a venture into which the church, to be triumphant, must enter to regain and restore what has been stolen, lost or forfeited.

If we believe in a sovereign God, we must believe

in a sovereign grace that forgives again and again and seeks to restore with gentleness and strength. This is a story of radical grace and radical forgiveness and radical restoration. In this field there is little competition but astounding opportunity to represent the heart of God for a hurting world.

Most losses have points of closure. Your losses and wounds remain painfully open but with the pain there is an exciting expectation that this episode one day will end in a bright new morning after nights of weeping. Earlier than that day it appears you are already a sharper instrument in the hands of God, a deeper and more able lover of God and the lost. We do not understand the whys of suffering but we can readily behold the riches that accrue from it. With the presentation of this most helpful book, my prayer is that the day will come when a restoration will take place and the sun will shine on smiling faces when righteousness will roll down like floods.

This is a story "to be continued" and one day, perhaps sooner than any of us expect, we will hear the rest of the story and even the sadness of the first part will be wonderfully transcended by "the rest of the story".

Dear reader, could I suggest that your reading might be accompanied by intercession for all involved in this moving and unfinished drama thereby enabling us all to share the joy of a coming morning.

Enjoy, weep, and pray!

Jack Taylor, President

Dimensions Ministries

Melbourne FL

ഏⓍ

INTRODUCTION

BY MARK ODOM

If you have grown up anywhere near the church, you are familiar with the Parable of the Lost Son. In Luke 15, there is the account of a young man who leaves his father's home with his share of his inheritance only to find himself dining with the pigs a short time later. In complete humility, the son returns to his father who, in turn, openly receives him in celebration. This story is the ultimate example of restoration and how the Heavenly Father wants to embrace us after we fall. This story is precious to me. I am the lost son. I am one who is being restored.

As a college student, I decided to follow the Lord with passionate abandon. I was involved in student leadership in campus ministry. I also led several Bible studies on campus. After graduation, I was married and became involved in a nondenominational fellowship where, in a short period of time, I was filling leadership positions again. My wife and I were involved in the worship team and led a home group in the church. As a family, we strove to seek the Lord and follow what we thought He was saying to us. Things were going well in my Father's house.

Then things began to change one small decision at a time. While we were deeply involved in our church, my life as a young professional exploded. At work, I seemed to have the Midas touch as everything I touched turned to gold. My wife remained at home with two small boys while I traveled the country on my very demanding business. As I continued to succeed at work, I spent less and less time at home and my wife and I started to drift emotionally and physically apart. In a short period of time, I found a coworker who would fill both of those voids for me. Instead of serving the Lord and loving my family, I was in the middle of an affair and a million miles from God.

My wife and I separated. Without disclosing the truth, I told my wife that we were on different life paths and that it couldn't work out. In my heart, I had to run from God to deal with the sin and guilt in my life. I knew His truth. I knew His promises. I even remembered the specific words He had spoken over me for my life, but I chose to run away. Regardless, God was faithful. I remember weeping in hotel rooms wondering how I got to this place. I heard Him call me back over and over, but I refused to listen. I had already been damaged, by my own failures. The greatest struggle I faced was the knowledge that God loved me, and yet I chose to fight His pursuit of me all the way into my own personal disaster. My life was destroyed, I had done it, and now it was too late.

After 6 months, I moved back in with my family, but the affair continued. One minute I wanted to run away from the mess I had made and reconcile with my wife. The next minute, I loathed her and tried to make sure she knew it. Despite how I treated her, her love remained constant. Finally, after two years of her daily unconditional love, I decided to expose the lie that I had been living. Unbelievably, my wife received me openly. I knew that if she could love me the way that she did, that Jesus could only love me more. I finally came home—not only to my family, but also to my Father's Home.

I have been fortunate. There were many in my church family who embraced me just as my Father and my wife did. Where I expected self-righteousness, I found a loving body of Christ instead. I had some dear friends who were committed to seeing me through the healing process. The problem then became accepting my status as a restored son. How can I ever serve again? Why would God ever use me after what I did to Him? Shouldn't I be disqualified? Like the prodigal, I exclaimed, "I am no longer worthy to be called your son (Luke 15: 21b)!"

I am on the Road to Restoration now. It is a hard path to travel down, but the healing that comes with each step brings a new level of strength that I would have never known. I still wrestle with those questions, but I am learning to walk in the grace that God has shown me. I am starting to see that His promises for me still stand, regardless of what I've done. Also, I am now in the unique position to share this lesson in grace with others who have also walked this path. God never gave up on me and my love for Him has grown as this grace assumes a greater depth in my life. I have walked in the depths of sin and I have heard the Father say "Quick! Bring the best robe and put it on him. Put a ring on his finger and sandals on his feet. Bring the fattened calf and kill it. Let's have a feast and celebrate. For this son of mine was dead and is alive again; he was lost and is found (Luke 15:22-24)." God's heart is not to fix you. His heart is to restore you to His house and His purpose for your life. All we need to do is come home and let Him do it.

Broken reeds come in many forms, as Danny explores in the pages ahead. Affairs, abandonment, loss, and even disillusionment can break us. A number of life experiences can cause us to run away. The best part is that the story can have a happy ending. In our return, our Father wants to celebrate. More than we can ever imagine, He rejoices when we come home. As you read on, may you find yourself being restored in whatever form your brokenness has come, and then may you help restore others who find themselves as broken reeds.

~ Mark Odom

CHAPTER ONE

THE PROCESS OF GRACE

*T*he Scriptures abound with accounts of those who somehow ended up outside of the intended purposes of God. The process of pointing these individuals back to their intended purpose is one of the most incredible evidences of grace that this world has been privileged to witness. Sadly, the church has often missed this powerful opportunity of the expression of Christ's love, and so the world observes a Christianity that doesn't understand brokenness and has no understanding of humanity.

.

It is apparent to many in the world that we, The Church, have simply wanted converts that make no mistakes, experience no disaster, and walk through life "clean" without blemish. To those watching on the outside, the church can be most hypocritical simply because there is no grace given for those who may need it the most.

I am not implicating all. There are some, a few, who have wielded the weapons in the right place, against the enemy who loves to oppress and restrain God's people and purposes. What excites me is that this number is increasing; my hope is that in the days to come this number will overshadow the failures of the church in the past.

Restoration is a process of Grace. It is the manifestation of Jesus in the life of failure, in the circumstance of failure, and in the presence of fallible humanity. Grace, which is to be seen by the world[1], throughout the generations, becomes the evidence of the kindness of God. When we ignore the narratives in the Bible depicting these incredible corroborations of God's mercy through the ages, particularly in our own Christian practice, we don't bring anything to the table to open the eyes of those who are unbelievers, because the blind are those who are trying to reach them.

It is a hideous error and personal spiritual blindness, to see a fellow believer as "washed up" without future purpose, or at least without future "designed" purpose. I believe that most who are "on the shelf" away from God's intended purposes and calling are a result of a church that has not learned how to restore, how to heal, how to "be confident that He who began a good work will complete it!" [2] It has seemed easier to find fresh blood who won't mess up than fix something that is very broken.

Interestingly, the world doesn't even do that with its

broken. Recently, in the news, there have been a number of highly effective company executives who have fallen on hard times. Some have experienced bankruptcy; others have chosen the failure by foolish decisions that resulted in a criminal conviction. Regardless, in each of these cases, the world continues to recognize their "gifting" and their "calling." It wasn't that their failure was without consequence, but their future is still intact as significant businessmen or businesswomen in the world where they found their "vision" being fulfilled.

At first glance, some might well say, we believe in restoration, just not the restoration you are talking about. We believe that restoration means a return to the original state. In the case of marriage, it would necessarily mean that a marriage would be restored to the original marriage. In the case of other areas of brokenness, it would mean a return to the original vision with everyone still intact.

If there is one thing that is certain, it is that this kind

of restoration is not ever a reality. Something always changes. I have a dear friend who experienced a phenomenal touch of the Lord in the mid 90's. He and his wife are dear friends of mine. He fell, absolutely, chose to... no excuses. He would tell you the same thing.

During that time, I remember reminding him of the purposes and destiny that God had for him. I reminded him of the supernatural events that had been so profound during that period of time in his life. A few months later, I heard that he and his wife had been restored. Was it the same? No. There were changes that had taken place in both of them. God was pulling about the purposes in them that He desired to be expressed.

Was it restoration? Absolutely! It was the kind of restoration that all of us are excited about, the kind of restoration that none of us would have a problem with... and yes, it was a restoration brought about by the Father in the lives of that couple.

But what if? What if the restoration doesn't happen like that? What do you do when others choices produce "points of no return" in relationships or in places where God has called you to function? Is there restoration there? Can a person experience the fullness of God's hope, promise, and destiny if Humpty-Dumpty can't be put back together?

I believe you can, and that is the foundational premise of this book.

I originally intended for much of this material to be addressed to a specific "church leadership" periodical to help leaders of a denomination respond to the issues that were confronting them. At that time, it seemed as if they were dealing with the reality of several leaders and other individuals who were making poor choices that were having significant ramifications on leadership, and also beyond leadership into the constituency of the churches.

It appeared that these leaders who were broken were simply cast off somewhere. I spoke to several who wept bitterly about the number of years they had given in service to their flocks and to this movement, and now they were Persona non grata, unwelcome, and alone.

After submitting the article, I received a phone call from the publisher who acknowledged that my article covered well a remedy for the growing problem in the movement. They indicated that they wanted to publish the article, but wanted to first contact a few of those mentioned in the article. They confirmed that the issue was a real one, but they hadn't heard a legitimate response to leadership, and they were contemplating the ramifications of an article like this one. One of those they contacted requested they not include the article because it was very incriminating towards him. The publisher complied out of deference to the pastor, and so the problem remained, as it does in much of the church.

My intent was not to incriminate, but educate. As leaders, we must be willing to look at our ability to restore broken leaders as well as develop new leaders with a frankness that will encourage growth and change.

The intent of this book is simply that. There is no malice I have for the church; I see the church as something Jesus died for, something that He is coming back for, and something that He has called me to pull into Her Destiny.

I believe that should we fail at, this most meaningful task of restoration, we will be breaking the bruised reeds that Scripture says are not to be broken. On the other hand, if we succeed in restoring those who have run into caves to hide in fear of the wrath of church leadership; if we succeed in restoring those who have fallen through choices made, whether that be their own, or someone else's; if we succeed at raising up old warriors who have the scars, fortitude, and maturity to face the worst battles;

then I believe we will be well on our way to seeing the Bride of Christ rising without blemish, without stain, wrinkle-free... in Glorious Strength and Power.

1 Ephesians 2:5-8 "...when we were dead in transgressions—it is by grace you have been saved... "God raised us up with Christ and seated us with him in the heavenly realms in Christ Jesus, *in order that in the coming ages he might show the incomparable riches of his grace, expressed in his kindness to us in Christ Jesus.* For it is by grace..." - italics mine

2 Philippians 1:6 "...being confident of this, that he who began a good work in you will carry it on to completion until the day of Christ Jesus."

CHAPTER TWO

THE GENERATION OF VICTORY

$\mathcal{I}$ have a hope that soon there will be a generation of those who will walk with Jesus in Power and Authority. I have a hope that these will be those who stand as mighty champions in this hour recalling the heroes of old who faced giants, fire, and persecution, but overcame by the word of their testimony and the Blood of the Lamb. I have a hope that these will take the helm of the ship and steer it towards victory and away from comfort because they know that victories are won in battlefields not in living rooms.

Victory is reserved for a certain type of person. The proud, religious and elite will never see victory. They may feel comfortable, safe, and peaceful, but they will never see true victory! Victory is reserved for the rebuked, the broken, the desperate, the "in-love," the frustrated, the extremists with nothing else to lose!

I know this because I've looked at those who are walking in victory around the world. They really aren't anything all that special. They're just deeply in love with Jesus and deeply passionate about living Him through their lives!

I have endured a few things in my tenure of life. Some think these things are disproportionate for me. I can only thank Jesus that He graced me with these events that let me see His Face and His wounds in a more real way.

I want to be like Paul who was able to say, "Don't you dare touch me, I've got the marks of Jesus branded on my body." [1] Amazingly, we live in a world that has taught us well the antithesis of a Biblical lifestyle. The more we hurt, the more we believe we are not under God's purposes. Nothing could be further from the truth.

We've branded the broken as unspiritual, or even in sin. Scripture seems to speak the exact opposite. Psalm 34: 18 tells us that "...the LORD is close to the brokenhearted and saves those who are crushed in spirit..." Maybe, just maybe, we should be hanging out with the broken, so we can see the heart of the Father more closely.

Are the broken the ones who get to bear the marks of the Lord Jesus in their body? It would seem so.

I've learned about restoration the hard way because I've had to walk through it. The first of these events happened while pastoring a church in the 90's and another occurred on the eve of the millennium. Both of those processes led me through my own trail of tears as I realized that the church was not equipped to handle my brokenness and the process of restoration that would be needed for me. I had never previously understood the passages I was now being forced to live. I had never equipped the churches I had planted and pastored for eleven years to handle the pain of my own life in that moment. But God was about to teach me invaluable lessons that would push me forward into His destiny for my life.

…a bruised reed He will not break!

"A bruised reed he will not break, and a smoldering wick he will not snuff out, till he leads justice to victory." Matthew 12:20

1 Galatians 6:17 "Finally, let no one cause me trouble, for I bear on my body the marks of Jesus."

CHAPTER THREE

RESTORATION OF A LIFE

B rothers, if someone is caught in a sin, you who are spiritual should restore him gently. But watch yourself, or you also may be tempted. Carry each other's burdens, and in this way you will fulfill the law of Christ.

(Gal 6:1-2 NIV)

"It seems as if all the holy men have gone off and

died and left us sinners to do the work of ministry"

(Jamie Buckingham)

The comment drove a dagger in my heart. "I'm really sorry but could you remove my name from all your literature, I don't have anything against you, I just don't believe I can support you or your ministry anymore."

The statement came from someone who I considered my closest friend. He was the pastor-colleague-peer who I trusted most, and his firm words helped me draw the conclusion that my mind had been telling me over and over again. I was washed up, not worthy to ever minister again, and certainly would never again pastor a church. That comment was repeated through many people, using different words and different actions to communicate the same thing. "I'm sorry, but the reality is, you are broken... and all the promises given by God, all the prophecies spoken into your life, and all the seasoning you've had in the presence of the Father is finished. It's time to look for a different career, because you won't ever minister again, and certainly not in my church!"

I had just gone through the most severe trial of my life. I was abandoned by my wife of seventeen years and she left me with four very broken hearted children. I attempted on many occasions to bring about reconciliation and healing, but to no avail. I subjected myself repeatedly to pastor after pastor, counselor after counselor, trying in any conceivable way to restore my marriage. This marriage was Humpty Dumpty all over again, and all the kings' men could not put it back together.

I remembered that passage in Judges 19 about the concubine who was raped and then left for dead. Her master then cut her up and sent her body to the twelve tribes of Israel. The response was "Such a thing has never been seen or done, not since the day the Israelites came up out of Egypt. Think about it! Consider it! Tell us what to do!" It seemed as if my marriage had been raped, and now my broken life was being ripped apart, and no one knew what to do or how to help. I couldn't believe I was experiencing such a painful ordeal, and the very ones I loved most were the ones hurting me the most.

I had been pastoring a church in our contemporary denomination for over ten years. I had been involved in the early inception of the movement that was often referred to as "the glory days" of the movement. I walked through the explosive releases of inner healing, spiritual warfare, and prophetic ministry. I went to churches that were exploding in renewal, in those early outpourings. I saw it and personally experienced the power of that renewal. I watched in awe as God released this precious outpouring in our church back home. I had done a flurry of conferences on small groups, healing, warfare, church planting, and worship. I began working with area churches in our movement and eventually became involved as an "Area

Coordinator." I also worked with many pastors in the city where I pastored and became involved in citywide ministry. Life was good. I knew what it meant to be to be fully immersed in our denominational life.

I watched the emergence of the movement and was so excited to be a part of something so world changing. I realized that much of the church in the western world had been transformed through conferences and worship in this movement and I was a part of the ministry that transformed it. What a blessing.

Then everything broke.

One hideous Sunday morning I was faced with the fact that I had been abandoned by my wife. Furthermore, not only was I abandoned, but my precious kids were abandoned as well. My youngest was a baby in diapers, and my kids were absolutely shattered. I remember many nights listening across the house to cries that went on for hours. I remember going through entire nights without sleep for five or six days in a row. I wept, I yearned, and I found a side of me that I never knew existed. I collapsed during that time into the abyss of sorrow, wondering if I would ever make it out.

During those days, my Dad who had been involved in ministry around the world for over forty years revealed to me one of the greatest truths that anyone could reveal during a time like that. I had just told him "Dad, I know the promises that God has made to me, but right now the pain that I'm going through far outweighs the hope of any promise. I'd rather just die." With tears streaming down his face he responded with great and humble wisdom, "Son, I don't know what to say, I don't know what to do to help you, but I love you!" It was enough to hang on to.

"But those who suffer he delivers in their suffering; he speaks to them in their affliction. " He is wooing you from the jaws of distress to a spacious place free from restriction, to the comfort of your table laden with choice food." (Job 36:15-16)

One of the greatest tragedies that I witnessed during that time, and have since seen multiplied over and over in the church is the tragedy of how the church responded to me during my crisis. (I hold no ill feelings over that, I know that God allowed it and as a result have been able to help many who have walked through similar tragedies). I couldn't believe how those who were my "friends" and "colleagues" abandoned me. Those who I looked to for help and advice were not only hard to find, they vanished. They didn't call, they didn't try to help. They just withdrew. Members of my own staff became vocally critical of me, and withdrew support. There were numerous pastors of my own denominational movement who simply offered help on a ten-foot pole, telling me to do things that were ridiculous for a man in my condition and having to care for four children.

It didn't seem to matter to anyone that my brokenness was a result of someone else's decision. In their eyes, I was to blame for my state of brokenness.

Frankly, I learned very quickly that no one had answers to help me through. No one knew how to "restore" such a one, and no one liked being around leaders that had fallen.

Granted, I fell. But I didn't choose to. I was tripped. It wasn't my bad decisions or moral failure, but I was down for the count.

There are so many younger and older leaders who have walked away from the very calling of God, because leaders in the church didn't know how to restore them, and so they avoided them. What an indictment on the power of the Gospel. What an indictment on those who have received the fullness of the Spirit with power. What an indictment on the churches ability to "restore such a one."

It was amazing. During that time, I saw something I had never seen before. I realized that as a leader in my denomination I had actually perpetuated the ideology that "there is nothing out there like our movement." I had limited my scope of ministry to that which looked like, smelled like, walked like, talked like our movement. If someone came who was not a part of "us" they couldn't teach, preach, pray, worship, or do ministry at all in the church I pastored. I realized that I built exclusivity in the people that I pastored and I was not alone. There were many of my peers who taught and practiced the same thing. I believe it was that very denominational thing that made it impossible for others within the denomination to help in the restoration process.

How can a leader end up like this? It ruins the whole mix. Our leaders must be perfect. Their families must be absolutely whole. If they are to be a part of this movement we can't have a mess surrounding their life.

I took a Sabbatical and withdrew into the caves.

ॐ

David left Gath and escaped to the cave of Adullam. When his brothers and his father's household heard about it, they went down to him there. (1 Sam 22:1 NIV)

From across the room this older man almost ran into my face and shouted. "Danny, it's time to come out of the caves! God has a call on your life, and it's not to be set aside! Come out of that cave." Another charismatic Baptist pastor smiled at me and said, "You have words of life for people in this room, prophesy now!"

My knees were melting under me, I knew they were right but I was so hurting, I was so deep in the cave, I didn't know if I could come out. About a week later I was in a worship conference where the Lord manifested Himself incredibly. After about six hours of worship I was leaving when the wife of a prominent prophetic leader came to me and said, you need to tell my husband what you went through. As I approached him, he saw me, and before I could say anything, he said "Brother, you have not failed, you are not disqualified. God is going to use you!" As I looked at him, I could see the presence of the Lord all over him. I knew that what he was saying were not his own thoughts... but the thoughts of the Lord towards me. When he said those words I broke. The Lord began healing me and restoring me. The next night I witnessed as this leader demonstrated full restoration by giving the meeting to a former fallen leader of international exposure. He was busy restoring the fallen. Just a week later I received a phone call at midnight from another pastor outside our denomination who I didn't know in New Jersey. His statements were healing to me. He said, "You don't know me. I met you once with your friend John. I got your phone number from him. I've been praying for you for the past three weeks. When I sleep, I've been dreaming about you. When I spend time with the Lord, He's been telling me things about you, and even though your marriage will not make it, and you know that, YOU ARE NOT DISQUALIFIED, God is going to use you. All the gifts that He has given you in worship and teaching and ministry are still there, and you will fulfill His purposes for your life!" He spoke to me for about two hours. He shared the Lord's heart for me and healing was well underway. I was coming out of the caves!

ഔന്ദ്ര

"For my thoughts are not your thoughts, neither are your ways my ways," declares the LORD. "As the *heavens are higher than the earth, so are my ways higher than your ways and my thoughts than your thoughts. (Isaiah 55:8-9 NIV)*

Divorced.... what a weird feeling. All these years you've been married to this person, and all of a sudden they are no longer a part of your life. I had several divorced people in the church I pastored, but I don't think I really ever considered that God would give them leadership in any significant way. I mean, they were divorced. I let them do some things, they could work with kids, or help out in a home group, but giving them "real" leadership, I don't think so. I mean, they must have done something wrong, something that they didn't need to do in order to be in the plight they were in. Surely they circumvented the purposes of God and now would have to live with ramifications. That is really what I thought. And now, I was divorced.

Someone stood me up in a meeting and said, "God is restoring your life!" Then folks would gather around and say, "What a great word, I guess your marriage isn't really over!" But it was, and I knew it. They just didn't know how God could possibly restore a life in another way. To all of us in the church, an effective, loving, and faithful marriage is a supreme standard that we rightfully set on those called to minister. If "marriage" is the highest goal for someone in ministry, how could ministry ever be completed unless that was restored?

But God was restoring my life. He was restoring my life in ways that confound our ways. One of the things that we fail to see is that God restores us through means that are His prerogative to use.

☙☞

"Then I will make up to you for the years That the swarming locust has eaten, The creeping locust, the stripping locust, and the gnawing locust, My great army which I sent among you. "And you shall have

plenty to eat and be satisfied, and praise the name of the LORD your God, who has dealt wondrously with you; then My people will never be put to shame. (Joel 2:25-26 NASB)

I had four children without a mother. I had to support my family, but really had no skills that could sustain us, particularly with taking care of my kids. I had been abandoned while my kids were being home-schooled. Now that became a part of my every increasing responsibility. How could God restore me to what He called me to do? In my case, the Lord brought a precious woman of God. Her name was Karen. After enduring a difficult divorce and loss of her marriage a few years before, she had for some reason the ability to look at my situation, and see God's call on my life. Then she realized that God's call on her life was to me, to love me, and even love my kids as her own. (She brought three children with her).

We were to be married, but finding a pastor to marry

us was brutal as well. Who wants to perform the ceremony of a former leader? But there was someone who believed in us. Remember that Baptist guy? He saw that God's destiny for my life was not over and without hesitation wanted to bless the process that would help me reclaim that destiny. He willingly and lovingly performed the ceremony that would continue the restoration of my life!

After we were married and joined our families into a picture of nine (seven kids) we began to pursue God's calling in earnest. At first it was simply trying to figure out where to go, what to do. There were many former peers who would have nothing to do with me. I didn't have a huge list of folks to help me out. But there were three, three very precious men who never let the ball drop, who always loved me, and who always believed in me!

One of them was a businessman. He had been crucified by the church before, but really believed that God called him to invest into eternity with his profits. He chose to invest in me and literally paid me a salary for over a year. The church I pastored for over ten years had given me one-month severance pay, which was not very much for a man with four kids. Another man was a pastor friend who often would just check up on me. He encouraged me that if the Lord ever spoke to me about being with him on staff, to say the word, and I could come. The third man was that charismatic Baptist guy. What a man of integrity. During my broken time he challenged me repeatedly to stay true. He pled with the leadership of the church I pastored to not let me resign. He brought many citywide pastors around me to pray for me. He publicly responded in love and concern for me. He let me lead worship in his church with his team and let me preach from his pulpit. He began sharing my name with others so that I could have ministry opportunities elsewhere. He walked me through my darkest days. He suggested me to a church for consideration as a pastor. He believed in me and because of God's grace through him and others, I'm not resigned to never have "God's best" for my life. I believe that God's best is still there for me to apprehend, and some of it is being experienced today.

After our wedding, we sought out different ways to become effective in ministering to people. We realized that God would bring many hurting people into our lives, and we began a home group that quickly grew and became a lifeline for not only us, but also to others as well. We did some interim worship leading at a church about two hours away. It was healing, but could not have occurred unless that pastor believed in us and the fact that God was going to use us. We spent over a year just doing worship always knowing that God had more for us to do in the days and years to come.

The biggest key for the church to remember in dealing with leaders is that if God called them, He believes that they can fulfill what He has called them to do. Our focus should be more on restoring them to that which God called them to do, than on disqualifying them from ministry. Leaders, although not naive, need to be those who look at each other, realize the frailty of life, and believe in each other. Sure, there will be difficult things to walk through. Some of my earlier friends can't picture me with my precious wife Karen, but I wish they could. Some of them can't face the fact that life sometimes gives "bum deals" but it does, and I got one. I'm not complaining because God has had a purpose in all of it.

I love the story of John Mark. He was one who stumbled. Later Paul didn't want him around but Barnabas knew that John Mark was salvageable. There are many, many John Mark's out there. Many who have stumbled on their own, some who have been tripped by other's decisions, some who simply got nuked by the enemy. Nevertheless, they are needful for the church. They are needed not simply to fill a pew, but to proclaim and release the restoration of the Gospel of the Kingdom.

'For I know the plans that I have for you,' declares the LORD, 'plans for welfare and not for calamity to

give you a future and a hope. (Jeremiah 29:11 NASB)

I had learned very valuable lessons of what it meant to restore and be restored. Now I would face the most difficult of all restorations — the restoration of my heart!

CHAPTER FOUR

RESTORATION OF THE HEART

*J*t was Friday, December 17, 1999. My eldest son and his two younger siblings were going to spend a week with their grandparents in New Jersey. Their mother and uncle were picking them up. The pick up was uneventful. What followed continues to this day as the most painful of all events I would endure.

At about one o'clock in the afternoon on the next day, Saturday, the nightmare began for me. My eldest son, Peter, called franticly from a city he had never been to, where he was abandoned in a motel overnight. Without food, money, or a place to go, he called in extreme distress. "Dad, they took Christy and Abby. They're gone. It's my fault. I was sleeping!"

The words crashed in on my world with such a force I barely knew what to do. "Where are you now? Are you okay Peter? I'm so sorry. It's not your fault son! You don't have any money for food?"

After a few minutes I learned that during the night the girls were taken, the motel room that Peter and his uncle slept in was made to appear like there was still someone sleeping in the abandoned bed. Peter took a quick look over there earlier and didn't think anything of it. His greatest pain was the fact that he believed he was to watch over his two little sisters.

I quickly called the local police to meet my son at the hotel. He had been locked out of the room and couldn't get back in. I called the hotel and asked them to please find some food for him and I would pay them as soon as I could get there.

About an hour and half later I arrived in the city and found Peter weeping and in shock. Then the flurry of activity began. Police reports... FBI reports.... private investigators... missing children reports... lawyers maneuvering judges a state away to bring about some sort of remedy to this situation.

The courts had been warned of this possibility but ignored it as a spurious concern, and now they were seeing the reality of my concerns taking place in my life and the lives of my children. I had been granted full custody on several occasions with legitimate reasons. In fact, five separate court decisions had profoundly declared that the obvious welfare of the children was better suited under my care rather than in the emotionally and psychologically unstable environment of their mother. Now my concerns were fully realized.

The grandparents claimed innocence, even after they re-financed their home and couldn't explain where the money went.

My own world crumbled.

I had only recently been called to pastor a church in a rural area of North Carolina. Life was beginning to take shape again when this most hideous cruel event occurred. It wasn't simply watching another individual go through it. Not only was I going to have to walk through this event, my entire family was going to have to walk through another severe painful process placed cruelly on all of our lives through this kidnapping.

Here I was trying to pastor a church and yet again, life slapped me in the face! I didn't choose it. It came to me!

My anger in those days was horrible. I didn't understand how anyone could do something so cruel to two little girls. I actually received emails from individuals in the past who had been my friends and they said, "What did you expect after having gone through a divorce?"

I was totally aware of the fact that there were many who saw this event as a simple divine judgment on my own life. To them I deserved everything coming to me. How wrong they were. It was yet another lesson to learn in the process of restoration.

My precious daughters, caught in the kidnapping would now be subjected to years of living a life on the run, being given multiple alias names, taught that authorities were dangerous, taught to lie and deceive. The most hideous cruelty was to them! I wondered if these same self-righteous individuals felt that Christy and Abby deserved judgment too.

Even my older children bore the brunt of these critical comments. They had lost their siblings, and they had experienced the ripping and tearing of that loss out of their lives too! Comments from some graceless zealots drove daggers in their hearts too. Did they also deserve this cruel event?

I suppose this anger directed towards me by some of these individuals was a result of the fact that while I had been their pastor, my life fell apart, I was left broken and it hurt them. My devastation caught them off guard. In their minds, I was a leader who was never supposed to be so broken that I couldn't be fixed. How could they have been so foolish to follow a fallible human?

I walked through hope deferred more times than I can count. I dealt with so many leads, so many "prophetic" dreams and words that really held no "instant" value. I devoured the Word looking for promises that would grant me peace but I remained extremely broken through the process.

One day my precious wife Karen asked me to retrieve something from the girls' room. Twenty minutes later she came looking for me when I didn't return. She found me collapsed on their floor in inconsolable tears.

Many days I spent simply sitting in front of a blank screen on the computer trying to figure out something that I could possibly do to find my children. The emotions were overwhelming, and yet I knew I couldn't resign from the hope that I had that they would return.

A year after they were taken, my youngest son, Elijah was born. That morning I awoke with a song that would express so much of my heart in regard to my missing little girls, but it didn't bring them back. The words reflected the agony of my loss:

I went into your room today
I noticed everything in place
I saw your toys were in their box
Your clothes all put away
Your bed was all made up
Your books all stacked up right
I'm expecting you soon
To come and live here again

I expect you
I look every day
My heart cries for your presence
In the house that is your home
I expect you suddenly
To appear at my front door
Saying words I've longed to hear
Daddy, I've come home

I'm expecting you to run to me
To say I've missed you so
Can we go out and play now
The games we played before
Daddy, will you hold me close
And wipe tears from my eyes
I've missed so much of life with you
I want the pain to subside

I expect you
I looked for you today
My heart cried for your presence
And I long to be with you
I expect you suddenly
To appear at my front door
Saying words I've longed to hear
Daddy, I'm home...
Daddy, let's go play

It's been so long since you were taken
So long since you've been gone
But I know that you are coming
I know it won't be long

Till the coming is celebrated
And you are in my arms
I expect you oh my little ones
I expect you any day
My God has made a promise
And He will not delay

You are coming
You are coming
I expect you
The years that we have waited will covered in
years of joy
I expect you
I expect you

A few months later I received a phone call from Oregon, "Mr. Steyne, I'm the Sheriff in Joseph, Oregon. I believe your girls are in our area. I'm going over there right now. I'll be in touch."

Finally, my dreams were going to be fulfilled. Finally, my children were going to be restored. Finally, those who took them would receive the wrath of justice! About two hours later I received a second phone call telling me that someone had informed the abductors ten days prior and tipped them off. They were long gone. Five photos were all I had to confirm that, yes, it was them and they were growing up so fast! My heart broke, and once again my hope was deferred and my heart grew weary with sickness.

Media blitzes, national and local television appearances, magazine articles, IRS publications, and even a decal on a racecar produced no leads. I began to wonder if I ever would see those precious little ones again.

During that time I received thousands of emails and letters from all over the world, in fact sixty-five different countries. The little website that I had built one night in exasperation received about 150,000 hits. But still no Christy and no Abby.

One day I was sitting next to Karen, my precious bride. We were having a nice conversation unrelated to the girls when she blurted out, "Honey, I've really been praying about the situation with the girls. Maybe you should just release them to the Lord in this situation. What would you do if the Lord wanted them to be in the custody of Joyce right now?" The words hit me like a ton of bricks. Karen had never said anything close to that before. This was either God or something very wrong had happened to her. Would God require me to simply let this thing happen and trust Him?

I didn't respond but the hook of God was in my heart. I knew there was more to this picture than I was seeing. I began working on forgiveness but the process was slow. I forgave to the extent that I knew, but I knew that God would bring about retribution and that made me feel better.

๑๑

..."Like water spilled on the ground, which cannot be recovered, so we must die. But God does not take away life; instead, he devises ways so that a banished person may not remain estranged from him. "(2 Samuel 14:14).

The words were like the finger of God thumping on my chest. "Danny, you have thought because you were hurt by Joyce that I wanted vengeance on it, but I really don't. What I want is for her heart to be turned to me. You can't do anything over the past, but I absolutely want her restored to me."

I had never seen it that way before. For the first time I think I really understood what it was when Jesus said, while hanging on the cross, "Father, forgive them, they don't know what they are doing!" God didn't simply want me to release her; He wanted me to call into being the process of restoration by my words. He wanted me to begin to ask Him to break through the estrangement so that she would no longer feel banished from His Presence. I had come to Jordan of forgiveness and was ready to cross into the promised land of freedom.

I realized that for the previous several years I had carried around these two who had taken my children everywhere I went. I woke up with them on my mind, I went to bed with them on my mind. My meals, my relationships, my work, my recreation, everything was tainted with their presence. I had hated them with a perfect hatred but now God was asking me to forgive them with a perfect forgiveness.

I knew my only option was to fully release them and I let forgiveness flow. When I forgave them, I released them to God's purposes, and found myself back on the road of fulfilling God's destiny for my own life as well.

It took me time to work through that process of forgiveness. It took several years for it to be complete. In May of 2003, the Lord granted me the grace to respond with kindness and total forgiveness and release the girls to His Purposes. I sent a letter to Joyce's family. They read it, but wouldn't respond. I posted it on the internet. I told them they were forgiven—all of them. That all of the mess was in the past and that I hoped God would touch and bless each of their lives.

Something wonderful began happening to my thoughts. I realized that my Christy and Abby may have been set apart to be "Josephs" who would one day be the source of God's Grace for many as a result of their own journey. I realized that the impact on their lives, on Peter's life, in fact on all of our lives could result in the greatest measure of Grace we had ever known. My son Peter amazingly walks without bitterness, embracing the brokenness that came from that event, and knowing that God has a purpose for his life through the trials he has walked.

The events of the past several years had accrued a significant legal debt, one that I knew would take years to pay off. I had sought for ways for this debt to be released. A day after I sent the letter forgiving them, I received a letter from the largest of these creditors indicating forgiveness towards me for the debt I owed them. I was blown away. I had stepped into the Lord's Favor and I never wanted to leave it.

The Lord began teaching me that restoration is all about forgiveness, trust, and faith that He has a plan that will be fulfilled. My heart had to be restored and forgiveness was the fuel by which the Kingdom of Heaven brought about the freedom and healing I needed.

I now understand what it means when Jesus says

forgive seventy times seven. It's not for the sake of the person receiving forgiveness, but for the sake of the person giving it! When we don't forgive, we are bound to ineffectiveness, we are bound to fruitlessness, and we are bound to despair, depression, criticism, and judgment.

When we give forgiveness we are free. We are free to restore others and free to be restored!

CHAPTER FIVE

RESTORATION OF THE ACCUSED

*B*rothers, if someone is caught in a sin, you who are spiritual should restore him gently. But watch yourself, or you also may be tempted. Carry each other's burdens, and in this way you will fulfill the law of Christ.

(Galatians 6:1-2)

Now when Joshua was near Jericho, he looked up and saw a man standing in front of him with a drawn sword in his hand. Joshua went up to him and asked, "Are you for us or for them?" "Neither," he replied, "but as commander of the army of the LORD I have now come." Then Joshua fell facedown to the ground in reverence, and asked him, "What message does my Lord have for his servant?"

(Joshua 5:13-14)

"Danny, you know that if you hang out with that guy, many of the others are going to have a difficult time with you, you are going to ostracize yourself from the major pastors in this city!"

The words were reminiscent of earlier words where I had walked through a difficult season of life. Others withdrew from me because of events that unfolded in my family that weren't very pretty. I recalled that time as "the time all my friends abandoned me!"

This brother had been through it all. It seems that he wasn't a perfect pastor, and had made some pretty poor choices at critical times that resulted in some parishioners getting angry with him. But then there were the variables. The rent had tripled on the church facility they had from the owner for no apparent reason. A longtime partner in ministry devised ways to bring about this pastors' demise. A prominent leader in the church didn't want their sin to be called sin. And finally, the well-known speaker who came in and managed to hide the fact that he was living in adultery. All of these events came within months of each other, and it seemed apparent that favor had withdrawn from this pastor.

I would be foolish to believe this brother was perfect. I know myself. I know many others and amazingly God made us all human! I am sure there were things he did that were not exactly right, but perfection is not the mark of Grace, God's Presence in a less than perfect life is! God had and has a destiny for this brother. It is the mark of a believer, and a mark of a leader, to restore, heal, and encourage this brother towards the goal of His Destiny in Jesus.

Restoration. It's a difficult process. It could cost you relationships, it could cost you reputation. Hey, for Jesus, it cost Him His life! And yet restoration is the irrefutable heart of ministry for us as believers. It is the coupe de grace that God will reveal to the ages, of His great and powerful love at work in all of our lives. The Apostle Paul describes this in Ephesians 2:7. *"In order that in the coming ages he might show the incomparable riches of his grace, expressed in his kindness to us in Christ Jesus."*

Restoration is the prerequisite of the Lord's return. It is the evidence His presence in our midst. It is the fulfillment of His destiny in our lives and in the lives of those around us. If I can be so bold, it is what happens when God is in a people, because it is the evidence of Heaven on earth. For some reason Jesus is confined and restrained from returning to earth until everything is restored. *"He must remain in heaven until the time comes for God to restore everything, as he promised long ago through his holy prophets. (Acts 3:21)*

Evidently, God sees the ministry of restoration as most important for the fulfillment of His ultimate reveal, and yet it seems as if the ministry of restoration is least on the agenda of our attention. Rather, we have often found ourselves in the mire of criticism, judgment, opinion, and allegations. These four attitudes prevail in many of our lives as "discernment, wisdom, correction, and righteousness" but really have nothing in common with God's purpose for restoration.

Who is the real enemy? Where does he hail from?

ℰᏒ

"Then I heard a loud voice in heaven say: "Now have come the salvation and the power and the

kingdom of our God, and the authority of his Christ. For the accuser of our brothers, who accuses them before our God day and night, has been hurled down." (Revelation 12:10)

Real victory comes when accusation is hurled down! The heart of the Father is bent towards the broken far more than our attempts at human self-righteousness can achieve through criticism, innuendos, and judgments.

Maybe, just maybe, the heart of the Father is revealed through the pages of His Book. *"Then I saw this pastor, this Christian leader, who was so broken and fallen, finally standing before the angel of the LORD, and Satan was standing at his right side to accuse him. (I actually had a few things to say too!) BUT THE LORD said to satan, "The LORD rebuke you, satan! The LORD, who has chosen this one, rebuke you! Is not this man a burning stick snatched from the fire?"*

Now this pastor was wearing a lot of repulsive and filthy clothing that didn't seem to be fitting for the very Presence of God. To understate it, he was broken, and dirty, and seemed like he had really messed up his life, but there he was standing before that angel in all his filth and humanity.

The angel said to those who were standing before him, those who were "spiritual," those who were close enough to see and realize the humanity and failures. They were the ones he spoke to. He said "Take off his filthy clothes." Then he turned and said to this pastor, "See, I have taken away your sin. I've removed the past from you. I no longer count it against your future. I no longer remember the frailty of your human failures. Furthermore, I will put rich garments on you. Garments of destiny. Garments of your future. Garments of all that I have proclaimed over your life from eternity past. Satan thought he could destroy you through accusation by ostracizing you and causing others to find you contemptible, but He failed, because my Restoration always prevails!" (It reminded me of another man who ate pig slop and was embraced by a Father who gave him his own robe to cover his filth!)

Then I said, "AH HA, Did you see that? Did you see what the Father did for this man? It's time to prophesy life to him again. It's time to bless him! Father can I join in with blessing what you are blessing? Will Heaven join me in the celebration of this restoration if I give this man, whom so many have loved to hate, a word of encouragement and hope?

"Put a clean turban on his head." So they put a clean turban on his head and clothed him, while the angel of the LORD stood by and watched—and smiled—and rejoiced—because this man was NOW in the place of his destiny! This man was now clothed in his destiny. He was empowered for His Destiny!!! (See Zechariah 3:1-5 paraphrase mine)

I once heard a seasoned messenger of God say, "The reason God hasn't given the church discernment is because they would use it to criticize and destroy each other!" I absolutely know this to be true, both personally, and by observation. It is the rare servant who will use discernment to assist and help the brother who has fallen, has stumbled, and who is nowhere near the destiny that God intended for their life. Nevertheless, that is the call of God for us as believers.

"Brothers, if someone is caught in a sin, you who are spiritual should restore him gently. But watch yourself, or you also may be tempted." (Galatians 6:1) The focus for most has been the "watch yourself" not the "restore gently" and as a result many unrestored lay in heaps by the side of the road, waiting for some "good Samaritan" to come to their aid.

It's pretty obvious that people whose reputations have been damaged no longer enjoy the favor and attention of the "righteous." They have become blemishes and could contaminate the good reputation that these self-righteous may have. At least that's what I've been told. And it is certainly what I have witnessed. A well meaning Christian can become guilty by association; they can become "tainted" by the hand that they are trying to restore!

I love Jesus. He is so un-pharisaical. He is so radically committed to this process of healing and restoration in people's lives that He does not care what others think about Him in His practice of the Father's Heart!

It seems that Jesus was not interested in earning either a reputation or a crowd! In Matthew 11:19 Jesus Himself portrays the attitudes of others who have judged Him. *"The Son of Man came eating and drinking, and they say, 'Here is a glutton and a drunkard, a friend of tax collectors and "sinners."' But wisdom is proved right by her actions."*

In the story of the man who was wounded and lying on the side of the road, the favor of God rested only on the one who did the Father's Heart. It was the Samaritan man, the least likely of all, who picked up, carried, helped, comforted, healed, and restored the fallen, broken man.

The story was never about us in the first place. It's not my reputation that matters. If Jesus could make of Himself no reputation (Philippians 2:7), then what on earth am I trying to do by making a reputation for myself. I would much rather follow His example than any other footsteps, ministry, church, pastor, or friend!

Because He willingly associated with the broken, we also have been invited to do the same thing. We are called into this ministry of associating with the broken, with the warriors who once wielded swords, but now only have the ability to nurse their wounds. *"All this is from God, who reconciled us to himself through Christ and gave us the ministry of reconciliation: that God was reconciling the world to himself in Christ, not counting men's sins against them. And he has committed to us the message of reconciliation." (2 Corinthians 5:18-19)*

Hang out with the broken. Hang out with the ones who no one wants to hang out with—you might find Jesus there! You might find His ministry there!

You see, to "restore" someone; means to absolutely bring them back to the place of their destiny and cause them to be fit again to do that which they are for! This is the ministry we've all been called to, but yet so often run from for fear of being labeled or ostracized or or or…..

I love the ministry of Jesus. I just absolutely can't find a greater example of any ministry that touched everybody. To those who thought they had "it" he made sure they knew that He didn't think they did have "it." To those who had nothing, he made sure they knew that they had everything. Blessed are the poor. Blessed are those who suffer. Blessed are those who thirst. Blessed are those who hunger.

The ministry of Jesus has always been a ministry of reconciliation and not a ministry of condemnation. That is the ministry we have been called to. It's a ministry of reaching out to the broken, to the barren, to the fallen, and to those who may have even experienced a season of "fame" next to us. Somehow through their own decision or the decisions of others, or simply because we all live in a fallen world, they ended up existing in the unenviable place of "outside the camp."

These are the ones I want to hang out with! I think Jesus hangs out there! I think we can sense the very robes of eternity walking through our midst when we have no fear that others will judge us. Because we know the One who judges justly, and He did restored the broken too!

I call them bones. Once with flesh, once with life, once with purpose, once living in the destiny to which they had been called. They have now become apparently devastated, without hope, without life—even the marrow has dried out!

I love these bones. These bones represent to me the most significant of all miracles in the Bible. They represent to me the army that couldn't breathe that becomes the army that will overcome, overpower, overthrow the gods of this age, and breathe life into this world!

Listen to the words recorded by Ezekiel in pertaining to the washed up, the used up, the never again, the devastated, the useless, the broken, the fallen, the dried out!

"The hand of the LORD was upon me, and he brought me out by the Spirit of the LORD and set me in the middle of a valley; it was full of bones. He

led me back and forth among them, and I saw a great many bones on the floor of the valley, bones that were very dry. He asked me, "Son of man, can these bones live?" I said, "O Sovereign LORD, you alone know." Then he said to me, "Prophesy to these bones and say to them, 'Dry bones, hear the word of the LORD! This is what the Sovereign LORD says to these bones: I will make breath enter you, and you will come to life. I will attach tendons to you and make flesh come upon you and cover you with skin; I will put breath in you, and you will come to life. Then you will know that I am the LORD.'" So I prophesied as I was commanded. And as I was prophesying, there was a noise, a rattling sound, and the bones came together, bone to bone. I looked, and tendons and flesh appeared on them and skin covered them, but there was no breath in them. Then he said to me, "Prophesy to the breath; prophesy, son of man, and say to it, 'This is what the Sovereign LORD says: Come from the four winds, O breath, and breathe into these slain, that they may live.'" So I prophesied as he commanded me, and breath entered them; they came to life and stood up on their feet—a vast army. Then he said to me:

"Son of man, these bones are the whole house of my people. They say, 'Our bones are dried up and our hope is gone; we are cut off.' Therefore prophesy and say to them: 'This is what the Sovereign LORD says: O my people, I am going to open your graves and bring you up from them; I will bring you back to the land of your destiny. Then you, my people, will know that I am the LORD, when I open your graves and bring you up from them. I will put my Spirit in you and you will live, and I will settle you in your own land. Then you will know that I the LORD have spoken, and I have done it, declares the LORD.'" (Ezekiel 37:1-14 NIV)

There it is. The people that will rise up as the army are not the ones who are perfect. They aren't the ones who have managed to avoid all appearance of death. Rather, they are the ones who have walked through the valley of death.

These are the ones who found that there, in that awful place, the One who is close to the brokenhearted, the One who loves raising the dead, the One who hands out the ministry of reconciliation and restoration, has given them their destiny back. He has brought them to a place of victory, power, and fullness because they have walked directly into the battle.

They have already died and their reputation is meaningless now. They perceive that their accomplishments of the past are merely works of the flesh because they have died and their life is now hidden with Christ in God. Indeed, they are the walking dead men and women.

.

They are the army of Ezekiel. They are the Army of Joel that strikes fear into the heart of the enemy, because having been slain, having been in the crucible of fire and death, they loved not their own lives, but retained the life of God in them. They will rise as an army that knows that God is faithful, that God sustains, that God restores, and that God gives hope. God has placed them back in the destiny that He ordained from the foundations of the earth, because the story was never about you or me, but GOD who is all and in all, and through whom we live and breathe and have our being!

The story is about Him, and He has chosen the foolish to confound the wise. He has chosen to give us this ministry. He has chosen to take the weak things. He has chosen an Army of Bones, against the counsel of the Pharisees, against the counsel of the naysayer, against the counsel of the self-righteous, and against the counsel of the self-proclaimed prophets of purity!

To those of you who are the broken: He has chosen you, oh dry bones! He has chosen you. Stand up! It's time for life to come back into you. Stand up! It's time for you to be restored to your destiny. Breathe in! Feel once again eternity, destiny, and purpose fill your life and be restored to the place God has called you to walk in.

To those who willingly stand in the way of restoring

one who is broken: There is an army rising around you, but it's only made up of broken soldiers? It's time to fall on the Rock and be broken—*"Therefore I tell you that the kingdom of God will be taken away from you and given to a people who will produce its fruit. He who falls on this rock will be broken to pieces, but he on whom it falls will be crushed."* (Matthew 21:43-44)

The time of restoration is upon us! The Kingdom of Heaven is here! The army of Bones is rising!

CHAPTER SIX

GET BACK TO THE JORDAN!

*I*t has always been the heart of the Father. It always has been. Take a quick look at the Bible. Abraham, what a mess up! Moses, now that's incredible, a murderer who will become a leader! David how could you, murder and then lie to cover up your adultery? Peter, you liar, you coward! We really could go on and on!

The servants were all messed up. That's why God could show grace to them. The angels must be stunned to watch the things God does through broken and fallen humanity. Maybe that is the reason He does use fragile vessels, because He can!

The Jordan is the prophetic place of "verge." In order for promises to be fulfilled we must pass through this threshold, beyond this margin, and across this border. It is the place before destiny from which so many of us have been diverted from time to time. It's the place where the only answer is to go through. There are no shortcuts to God's Destiny for your life, there is only that place called Faith by which it pleases Him to part waters for you!

You may believe that you have passed by the Jordan many times. There never was someone to part the water for you. You may feel attacked and knocked down, but the Jordan remains. The gifts and calling of God are irrevocable and they rest on you alone! Your Jordan, can only be crossed by you (see Romans 11:29).

As I near the end of this book, my prayer for you continues. I pray that in seeing the heart of the Father and His great restoring love for you, you will resolve to press into His purpose for your life. My desire is that your grasp of this truth has pulled you to the place where you can get up, come out of the cave, and hear the still small voice of God say to you, "I am still for you, and I will complete all that I have called you to do!"

When you hear those words, you can know restoration is well underway, and the best is yet to come!

It is His Will for you to stand! It is His Desire that you walk into your purpose and destiny. Regardless of what you have heard from the naysayers, regardless of what you have felt in your own heart, regardless of the mountain you must climb to come out of your valley, His Destiny for you awaits. Today, I call you into that Destiny! Today, I pull you forward into the purposes of God for your life, for your future, and for the future of those around you!

CHAPTER SEVEN

FROM DEVASTATION TO RESTORATION

All this is from God, who reconciled us to himself through Christ and gave us the ministry of reconciliation: that God was reconciling the world to himself in Christ, not counting men's sins against them. And he has committed to us the message of reconciliation. We are therefore Christ's ambassadors, as though God were making his appeal through us. We implore you on Christ's behalf: Be reconciled to God.

2 Corinthians 5:18-20

They are out there, these devastated ones. They retreat to caves; they try and hide from exposure, usually inflamed by some in the church who prefer exposure, criticism, and judgment to healing, restoration, and life. I remember one day of profound significance that demonstrated to me the extremes of how critical this ministry of restoration and reconciliation is.

That day forever painted a picture on my heart of my own need to encourage, help, and restore my brothers and sisters. On the one hand I spoke to one very broken pastor well retreated into a cave. It took me over ten months, and probably fifty phone calls until he finally spoke to me. His wife would answer the telephone and simply indicate he did not want to talk. What a joy when he finally picked up the phone. I ministered love and restoration to him, I prayed for him. He indicated that he would like to get together and continue the process of a restoration into the destiny that God has for him. Restoration had begun.

But then there was another powerful minister of the Gospel. God has used him around the world in thousands of lives. His ministry impacted my own, and continues to be some of the most effective ministry that ever occurred in my life. There it was, in black and white, verified, true. He fell. My heart broke. How could this happen Lord? I knew that it is for such a time as this, that books like this need to be written.

This is not time to judge, not time to criticize, not even time to try and figure out what went wrong. This is the time to demonstrate the ministry of reconciliation. This is the time for many to touch the life of this man and redeem him. This is the time to call him back to his destiny and purpose. This is the time to "restore such a one" in humility, that

God's purposes would go forward in his life. It's time to roll up our sleeves and immerse this one with love and help, and not discard him as has been the practice in much of the modern day church. It is not time to broadcast the failing; it is time to invoke the Presence of the Living God into his life.

It is easy at any point to judge, the key is not to! It is also easy to ask questions without giving answers. I hope that this book has not only raised the right questions but also helped to give some tools to very real ministry throughout the church.

The Ministry of Restoration is the ministry of Jesus. It is the woman caught in adultery, Zacchaeus caught in embezzling, Peter caught in a lie, and the criminal hanging on a cross. Reconciliation is the mark of Jesus' mercy shown to those who in many cases deserve judgment. It is the grace, the covering over of love that invites fallen, broken, bruised people into a meaningful purpose and destiny.

Restoring someone involves loving them more than, and through, all the junk that might be afflicting their lives. It is having mercy, and living ongoing mercy and purpose daily in front of them.

Recently, I was with a man who has a tremendous heart for the poor. A decade ago, he and several other friends would venture out onto the streets to minister to feed the homeless. The ministry grew into a delightful small ministry.

A couple years later, another ministry came to town and essentially took over the focus of this little ministry and my friend ended up on the sidelines. I tried to involve him in the new bigger ministry, but it was not his vision or his heart. The missions were very different. His ministry died, although his passion and heart for the poor never did. A few years later the newer ministry also closed its doors.

This past winter I saw my friend again and I asked

him what he was doing with the poor. He replied that he was not really doing all he knew he should be doing on the streets. Basically, his ministry had occurred in solitude and he knew God had more for him. I asked him what he was doing with the call that is obviously on his life for that type of ministry. He told me that God had been speaking to him about that as well, but that he hadn't initiated it yet. He told me that several had encouraged him to go back to the streets, and that the Lord had told him that if he went back out, "the people will follow."

I responded to him, "I just want you to know that every time I see you I am going to call you back to the intended destiny of God in your life!" He did not really expect that. A month later, I again spoke to him of His destiny. God had been speaking to him through others and during prayer. A couple months later, he went out with a couple people into the streets with some hot dogs.

The first night they fed a small group of people. Since then, they have had crowds up to about two hundred people that they are serving weekly. There have been healings and deliverances, and we believe, that on at least one occasion, God has multiplied food supernaturally. My friend was back doing what he was intended for, and God was blessing it incredibly.

Several, including God, simply called him back to His Destiny. Restoration is like that. It is us, working with the Father, to bring about fulfillment, purpose, and vision in the life of a servant who is devastated.

ഇൻറെ

When they kept on questioning him, he straightened up and said to them, "If any one of you is without sin, let him be the first to throw a stone at her." Again he stooped down and wrote on the ground. At this, those who heard began to go away one at a time, the older ones first, until only Jesus was left, with the woman still standing there. Jesus straightened up and asked her, "Woman, where are they? Has no one condemned you?" "No one, sir," she said. "Then neither do I condemn you," Jesus declared. "Go now and leave your life of sin."

John 8:7-11

Jesus simply called this woman back to a destiny that He intended for her. His destiny for her was not condemnation, not judgment, but rather life with a very real purpose.

Our role as healers is to once again prophecy destiny into the lives of those who are broken. We are the only ones who can pull a generation of broken people out of the mire of despair, believing that God may never use them again. We are those who have been entrusted with the ministry of reconciliation, and it is not simply for the lost, it is also for the found who have lost their way.

While I was writing this book, someone asked me some very pertinent questions. "Danny, how are you going to not only give us a hope and promise that restoration can happen, but also help us initiate ministry where we can see people's lives restored? How can we carry a broken servant to the place where The Counselor and The Comforter has come and brought restoration? How can we bring healing into the person's life where they cannot only relate to the stories and illustrations that you have told, but also where they know they have entered into that Holy place of His Promise? How can we know that not only has healing begun, but transformation has taken place, where the reader will complete this book, not simply informed, but changed?"

The ministry of restoration is simple. It is love. Although Jesus will not break a bruised reed, many times in our self-righteousness we will. Recognizing that is the first step in becoming a restorer. When we consider our own self-righteousness and realize that God is full of Grace and Mercy towards the broken, we enter the role of being Restorers!

Restorers know that people can be knocked down, perplexed, persecuted, and hard pressed on every side, and still accomplish the purposes of God. [1]

And so, the role of the restorer becomes a primary role in the life of the church. Without restorers, the anointing, and gifting, and calling of many lay dormant. The effectiveness of the church is diminished without these precious people. The role of the restorer is the heart of the Father. In fact, one of the most incredible promises to God's people, is the promise that we will rebuild ruins and repair walls and be restorers of the streets where people dwell.[2]

When we take the rubble of broken lives and return them to the purposes for which they were intended, we fulfill that prophecy! To fail to embrace and enter into the ministry of restoration is failure to apprehend one of the most awesome promises of Scripture.

As restorers, we pull people back into their destiny. We do not wallow with them in the mire of their despair, although we love them when they are there. We constantly refer them to the prophetic words declared over their lives.[3] We call them back to the gift of God entrusted to them. We fan that gift in their lives, reminding them that God's purposes exceed our own failings, emotions, and despair.[4]

When everyone else around the broken person has declared them dead, a restorer will declare them simply asleep. A restorer simply sees the broken in a cave. The restorer sees a person in a moment of time where the pain of life, the failure of life, the crushings of life have become more real than the truth and power of God's purposes for their lives.

To those whom God has graced with the stewardship of his provision, be the one who steps in and says, "I believe in the purposes of God in you. Even though now it appears that everything is shattered, I will not abandon you. I will help you!"

Often those who suffer such devastation have no means for providing for their own lives or those of their families, and usually the emotional pain prevents them from functioning in what would be common for most individuals.

When someone is knocked down, crushed, perplexed, and feels like their future is gone, they have very little reason to work or to learn a new trade. Help them, not simply with words, but with kindness, with gifts, with the encouragement that Jesus has called them. Help them by sharing with them desire of God that they succeed in the restoration process. Their successful restoration completely into the purposes of God for their lives is also your successful fulfillment of God's purpose for you.

During my darkest hours, Mark and Nicole who wrote

the introduction to this book were my closest friends. That is what they were. They were simply friends. They could not relate to what I was going through, they did not need to. They simply loved me and cared for me. They always made sure that I knew they were there for me. That was enough.

People who have experienced something that has prevented them from accessing God's purposes in their lives need friends, not counselors, not fixers, not sermons, friends.

As a restorer, be a friend to the one who is broken.

Finally, as a restorer, wash them. Cleanse them with the healing of Jesus. Pray for them, not simply on your bed at night, but pull them into your hug, wrap your arms around them, and speak words of life to them. Lay hands on them, often. Recite, often, the prophetic words declared over their lives, and declare that our God is not a liar. Affirm the fact that He made no errors in choosing them for the purposes and callings that He entrusted to them.

Wash them with love. Invite them into your home. Visit them in their home, or cave, or place of hiding. Speak of them to your friends. Cut off criticism and judgment boldly, knowing the purposes of God for that person. It is the enemy who is the accuser of our souls... we are the restorers!

Break the mold of the religious spirit that says they will never accomplish anything again. Invite them to speak, share, and tell their stories or the things God is showing them in places where God can begin opening up their lives to His call again.

Be the one who will not let go, and will constantly declare his or her destiny alive, when everyone else has called it dead!

Then you will be called a restorer! Then you will carry

the mantle of Jesus who would never break a bruised reed!

1. (2 Corinthians 4:8-9 NIV) We are hard pressed on every side, but not crushed; perplexed, but not in despair; (9) persecuted, but not abandoned; struck down, but not destroyed.

2. (Isaiah 58:12 NIV) Your people will rebuild the ancient ruins and will raise up the age-old foundations; you will be called Repairer of Broken Walls, Restorer of Streets with Dwellings.

3. (1 Tim 4:14 NIV) Do not neglect your gift, which was given you through a prophetic message when the body of elders laid their hands on you.

4. (2 Tim 1:6 NIV) For this reason I remind you to fan into flame the gift of God, which is in you through the laying on of my hands.

CHAPTER EIGHT

EPILOGUE TO LEADERS

J am not easily fooled by religiousness anymore. I have walked both sides of the fence of leadership as a pastor and as one who has been broken, branded, and discarded.

I have no illusions of my past. I know my failures, weakness, and shortcomings, but I also know God.[1]

I have walked through a crucible where I can honestly say that God has opened my eyes to the arrogance I once had.

I remember a day when no divorced person could be a part of my leadership. I remember a day when I would look at a broken person and say "Get healed up, then you can serve!" I remember a time when I withdrew from those I had held close in my heart for fear of being sullied, for fear of being categorized, for fear of my own reputation.

No more.

Leaders, in this hour, the place where the hand of God is resting heaviest is on those who have been broken. Favor is on those who have walked through pain, and it is there that you will find your own favor too!

My hope is that you will take the message of this book and let it resource your heart with compassion for those whose hurts are far too deep to bear. It is my hope that you, along with many who are finding the heart of God throughout the world in the place of compassion, will take off the religious garb and take up the basin and towel to wash the feet of the Lord Jesus. Just as the woman who washed His feet with her hair, you too can express your love for Jesus through this ministry of restoration because "whatever you did for one of the least of these brothers of mine, you did for me." (Matthew 25:40)

Now go... restore the broken!

1 (Jeremiah 9:23-24) This is what the LORD says: "Let not the wise man boast of his wisdom or the strong man boast of his strength or the rich man boast of his riches,) but let him who boasts boast about this: that he understands and knows me, that I am the LORD, who exercises kindness, justice and righteousness on earth, for in these I delight," declares the LORD.

If you would like Danny Steyne or a Mountain Of Worship Team to speak at your church, ministry, or conference, or if you have interest in Mountain Of Worship, other MOWBooks, MOWMusic, MOWConferences, MOWRoundtable Summits, or Mountain Of Worship School of Worship, Creativity, & Ministry, please contact us at the address below:

the time has come

mountain of worship

when true worshippers will worship

Mountain Of Worship

P.O. Box 212204
Columbia SC 29221-2204
803-665-8990
www.MountainOfWorship.com
worship@mountainofworship.com

In 1987 I had a vision. I saw a flat plain that grew into a volcano and became a "Mountain of Worship" that exploded worship all over the region, the nation, and around the world. It was an event of passionate worship that resulted in exaltation, magnification, and praise of God in spirit and truth! It was full of God's Power and the miraculous power of God was released to all those in the shadow of the Mountain. This "Mountain of Worship" is not simply another organization it is not simply another noun on the "marketplace" of Christianity ... it is an organism and a verb... passionate about bringing Glory to the Father through "much fruit... it is a "perpetual event of spirit and truth worship". It is a lifestyle of worship. It is a region... a nation... the world ... abandoned to passionate holy worship... until every knee bows, every tongue tells, both the lost and the found, in heaven and in hell... that Jesus is Lord!